Tall Flowers and Living Long

Poems by
Mary Ricketson

REDHAWK
PUBLICATIONS

Tall Flowers and Living Long

Copyright © 2025 Mary Ricketson

All rights reserved. No part of this publication may be reproduced, distributed, or transmitted in any form or by any means, including photocopying, recording, or other electronic or mechanical methods, without the prior written permission of the publisher, except in the case of brief quotations embodied in critical reviews and certain other noncommercial uses permitted by copyright law. For permission requests, write to the publisher, addressed "Attention: Permissions Coordinator," at the address below.

ISBN: 978-1-959346-97-5 (Paperback)

Library of Congress Control Number: 2025940577

Cover Design (Art): Erin Mann
Book Design: Erin Mann

Printed in the United States of America.

First printing 2025.

Redhawk Publications
The Catawba Valley Community College Press
2550 Hwy 70 SE
Hickory NC 28602
https://redhawkpublications.com

For Finn

Every syllable sings in *Tall Flowers and Living Long*. Rose Creek comes alive. The doggies bark in time. The birds chirp and the sky changes in tune. Mary Ricketson's poems are inroads to humanity.

—Shelby Stephenson, N.C. Poet Laureate 2015-2018, NC Literary Hall of Fame since 2015, recent publications, *Nin's Poem, Slavery and Freedom on Paul's Hill, Shelby's Lady,* and *Praises.*

Experience the wonder and beauty of the natural world in Mary Ricketson's poetry book, *Tall Flowers and Living Long.* Hike the mountain trails and observe the lessons nature teaches us. "Come to Hanging Dog, see the farm…" Welcome the lovely showcase this award-winning poet offers. This amazing collection articulates her relationship with nature. Discover the peace and healing power of nature as Ricketson sifts soil with her fingers and finds "Garden Magic." The stirring collection will speak to your soul: "Trust the Earth when your wisdom falls…" This is a great gift for nature lovers and reminds us what we've lost in the hectic schedules of modern life.

—Brenda Kay Ledford, author of *Blanche*: *Poems of a Blue Ridge Woman* (Redhawk Publications, 2021).

Readers who enjoy the nuances of nature will savor Mary Ricketson's *Tall Flowers and Living Long.* She confesses her son calls her "a plant maniac." But not only plants. Early sections of the book focus on farming and flowers through the changing seasons and rhythms of everyday life. In Section IV winter arrives, along with death, and Section V highlights animals—dogs, mules, deer—who serve as our earthly companions. Ricketson's style is often clipped, and she relies consistently on imperative: "Be like a soft mountain mist" or "Stitch a piece of life to this mountain." But these gentle commands are also invitations—to a world of wonder, for which the poet offers, in the final lyric, a chorus of thank-yous.

—David Radavich, author of *Under the Sun* and *Here's Plenty.*

Table of Contents

I	13
Tall Flowers and Living Long	15
Community	16
Making Friends	17
Grateful	18
Potion	20
To Protect a Blueberry	21
Walnut Age	22
Sharing Spring	23
Garden Magic	24
Rising	25
Before the Rain	26
Spells of Beauty	27
To Darn a Sock	28
Trust the Earth	29
After the Night	30
Pieces of Hope	31
Rise to Comfort	32
My Handmade House	33
May	34
Tradition	35
Together	36
Forever	37
Strong Bones	38
Apple Pie and Kindness	39
II	41
Early Springtime at Home	43
Alive in Spring	44
Dog Named Magic	45
After Dogwood Winter	46

New Ways from Old	47
Tale of the Pink Lady Slipper	48
Beauty by Surprise	49
Sifting Kindness	50
Flow in Place	51
Spring Rain	52
The Storm	53
Good Year for Little Violets	54
Wildflowers	55
Father's Day	56
On the Farm	57
Honor	58
Marvel and Wait	59
III	61
Slow	63
Morning Prayer	64
Beautiful Wild	65
Summer	66
Before Breakfast	67
Decide	68
Rest	69
Luck	70
Instinct	71
Tending	72
Someone's Home	73
Deep in Summer	74
My Son Says I'm a Plant Maniac	76
Hope	77
Wonder	78
Tomato	79
Seeking Chanterelle	80

IV   81

Looking for Carolina Asters   83
Bold and Determined   84
Foggy Mountain Morning   85
Moon   86
Death   87
Summer's Gone   88
Daybreak   90
Go Back Outside   91
Winter Sun   92
Sprout a Plan   93
Thankful   94
Walk with Magic the Dog   95

V   97

Early Fall Walk   99
Getting Warm   100
Autumn   101
Mule in the Field   102
Teachers   103
Beautiful Brown Pair   104
Companions   105
Shaking the Blues   106
Walking   107
When Opportunity Calls   108
Light   109
Living as Things Are   110

VI   111

Cardinal Flower   113
At Home   114
An Old Dog   115

Numbered Days	116
Mystic of the Farm	117
Losing Mystic	118
After Rest in Peace	119
Lessons from Mystic	120
Beginning	121
Long Summer	122
Changes	123
Fog Lifts	124

VII   125

Neighbors	127
Cranberry Bread	128
Thanking Trees	129
On The Anniversary of My Short Marriage to a Man who Only Loved My Land	130
Winter	131
Still Sunshine and Moonshine	132
December Sun	133
A Natural Glow	134
Gone	135
To Sew the World into the Life you Own	136
Peace	137
Out in the Country	138
Held by Nature	140
Acknowledgments	142
About the Author	143

I

Tall Flowers and Living Long

Queen Anne's lace still stands.
Long season of brilliant white
atop tall stems set the mood,
abundant joy, alive day after day.
Some shrink and fade, call an end
to the season. Others last long,
on into forever. No one knows
the secret of lives living long.

Community

Here. Bond with nature
and with people. Share
needs and favors. Count
on trees, flowers, butterflies,
hawks and goldfinch.
blue sky, cold rushing creeks,
dogs, horses and mules.

Sally Belle the Arabian mule
stands tall in the meadow,
bends low to eat.
All her world is here, essence
of it all.

Now the sunbeams shine, light
up the day, hold what's needed,
shed the rest to float down creek,
away to nevermore.

Making Friends

To make friends with this land, walk the same path
every day, morning, mid-day, and just before dusk.
Speak to flowers in bloom. Count pastel petals,
remember the scent. Notice each weed up close,
discover new beauty. Be impressed with unexpected.

Call every tree by name. Learn what matters to its life.
Touch the bark, linger awhile. Watch leaves move
in a breeze. Stand under its arms, keep dry in a soft rain.
See where birds land on a limb. Find a nest if you can.
Let birds become your favorite music.

Appreciate new shallow flats of water where beavers
beveled leaks into the creek, flooded land you
used to hoe. Learn to love the change.

Plant a walnut sapling saved from the saw,
even if you might not be alive when it's grown.

Grateful

Come on down to Hanging Dog, see the farm.
Watch Sally swish flies with her mule tail
and wonder if it's enough breeze to help
in the late summer heat. Bend yourself, slurp
a handful of water from the spring.

Turn at the corner where stalks
of ironweed pop purple, taller than the glow
of goldenrod growing among green weeds.

Come around where bare roots of a big oak
tree hold the dirt bank and keep the road in place.
See the great beech tree open its arms to all.

Welcome to the land of ferns and berries,
broccoli, lettuce, tomatoes, and flower beds,
where little dogs run free in the woods.

Come to cool mornings and hot days.
Hear cicadas rattle a tune in the sky.
Watch Sally swish her tail, bend over
forever to graze and never hurt her back.

Silt sets up a dam across Rose Creek
after a string of storms. Fresh blooms
of purple morning glory say the hottest
days of August will crawl into September.

Orange jewelweed shines like treasure
among dusty roadside weeds.
Bumblebees still pollinate purple stalks
of great lobelia and viper's bluegloss.

Keep a clear path to the lane now.
Walk with ease past flowers, bees and trees
every morning, every noon, every night.
Don't ever give up, grateful for every day.

Potion

Magic of dragonflies mends,
sews threads spun of afternoon air.
Not one blade of grass moves
in the memory of stillness.

North star and full moon meld
night rays into comfort and hope,
travel by light on fairy dust,
heal at sunrise when you are sick.

To Protect a Blueberry

Early morning in the bare
light of this waning crescent moon,
frost lies on the field, danger
to innocent blueberry blooms.

Spray clear water
before full break of dawn,
give tender petals a chance,
slow down the thaw,
ease the way into day.

Pray for berries to flourish
in full sun when warm revisits,
chance for frail flowers
to bear berries in summer.

Walnut Age

This walnut tree watches me
for forty years, holds me up with
broad branches, confides to me
the ways of nature, good times
and hard, love, hope, and despair.

Rain, snow, hot sun, wildflowers,
food gardens, songbirds and hawks
follow one another in rhythm.
Windy days and starry nights
were born under the limbs
of this great tree, grew steady
and askew in summer's full leaf
and winter's naked arms.

Life decisions sprung, invented
at the base of this walnut bark.
Ideas climbed the tree like children,
peeked out over high branches
to see the world, shimmied down
to live under rule of earth and sky.

Now, while a plague covers
the ground, this steadfast walnut
takes sick, loses the battle, waits
for the saw.

Life on earth remains in peril,
waits for the ways of sky.

Sharing Spring

Pink cherry blossoms bright,
apples flower in white petals again.

A pair of bluebirds stops
at the house atop a silver pole,
ready to build a home.

Maples red their edges.
Grass greens up in clumps,
blades and clover entwine.

Moss turns shades, winter to warm.
Forsythia spikes gold sparks of sun.

Still the trail tree points north to a star.
A new moon starts a season of love again,
when the planets direct the earth.

Seven deer dance down the unplanted garden,
dart back into the woods when footsteps warn.

Garden Magic

Put that curly kale into good dirt,
mostly sun, a little shade.
Plant rosemary where herbs do best
then sage next section over,
well beyond that mound of oregano,
mother-gate of this garden.

Feel the soft spring soil sift
between your fingers. Follow unexpected
roots between roses and vegetables.
Tap an unseen scent when a strong wind
swishes around you. Imagine the sweet taste
to come when this garden reveals its fruits.

Bless the rain tonight, how it sprinkles
the wise place with no words,
casts a glimpse of what's been hiding
beneath the roses.

Rising

Those tall green stalks standing in shallow
creek water will rise to blooms of yellow iris,
exquisite lady of the season.

Already, scattered clumps of daffodils shine
beauty. Spires of forsythia flower-bells
inspire wild majesty along roadside edges.

This rain will bring on the cherry blossoms
in perfect yards and rise the water loving
iris, pristine petals who declare a place to be.

Look at the fog rise high, feather its way up
the mountain tops, clear above the mule
pasture, make way for sun rays to touch

your face, kiss the ground. Blueberry buds
begin to burst open today, and short shoots
of crested dwarf iris rise to promise.

Before the Rain

List of farm chores grows long.
Separate into before and after,
rain the dominate factor at play.

Duty leads way, rules the roster
into lists of most needed and least.
Moss lies still and green, purpose
passive on the bank, still essential.

Crows call before time for cover,
before all the chores are close to done.

But dogwoods bloom full flower.
Speckles of white decorate
woodland edges even in the rain.

The old dog runs again,
and life is all that matters.

Spells of Beauty

Wander an untamed path where violets bloom
among grass and clover, and sundrops sparkle
on purple petals, perfect scatter, color and surprise.

Skip along without a plan. Step in a hole
where moles and voles bore into dark dirt,
fall down and stay awhile where purple petals reign.

Mingle where chickweed thrives beside violet gems.
Watch a yellow butterfly feed among longspur petals.
Spells of beauty transform the willing mind.

Allow time, tend an unknown spirit in the wilds.
Violet blooms pass, their time is too short,
but then the daisies have their day.

To Darn a Sock

For my mother

Find a spool of heavy thread
or lightweight yarn
close to the color of your sock.
Thread your large yarn needle.
Decide again, this sock is worth saving.

If the hole is small in the heel,
if the sock is wool, a favorite color,
proceed with patience.

Find the used-up incandescent light bulb
in the bottom of your sewing basket,
saved for this purpose, like the one
your mother used to darn old socks.
Remember how she dreaded this too.

Sing one line of *I remember Mama*,
teacher of all things needle and thread.
Have a sip of tea, then begin.

Slip the light bulb inside the sock,
smooth those torn edges against
the glass oval. Gently sew back
and forth, weave a fabric patch,
fill all spaces, tie a knot and be done.

Slip your feet into your mended socks,
take a walk outside, thank the lush earth
and thank your mother in the sky.

Trust the Earth

When your wisdom seeker falls, courts
a dance with death, and you don't know
which way the light will shine next, and
winter stalls along 'til the start of spring.
Try to trust the earth.

Invite your inner self to live, seduce a deep
protective place to peek out, meet the earth.
Watch maple tree tips turn red and invoke
the warm pulse of early March.

Look for a red-shouldered hawk,
all puffed up. He reigns in place on a wire.
Tiny new buds show up on the old dogwood.
Specks of yellow predict full bells of forsythia.
Your brown cow stands in the familiar field,
watches blades of grass grow green.

Every new moon begins a chance to start
again, time to rouse the wisdom seeker,
find the source, guide with a candle flame
and dance with life when pink buds
start to swell on blueberry branches.
Trust the earth.

After the Night

Walk early in a light winter rain.
The morning bird cries, cries again
and again, unseen in the bare
branches of a pear tree by a creek.

Walk this grief, constant of humans,
animals, birds and all creatures.
Walk the loss, the pain, the tears.
Walk the lines that sever and abandon.
Creep through remains.
Grapple step by step.
Every loss lines up to be greeted again.

Live in the crazy abyss.
Wait for a new cadence to seep in
after the rain.

Pieces of Hope

Put on your best smile,
one that starts deep inside,
spreads out wide as arms.

Believe your friend can live.
Nurture her to health
till life lives on its own surge.

Breathe blends of song
and prayer till her own breath
comes back, ease and harmony.

Blackbirds call, tucked
invisible in treetops.
Hear how they beckon belief.

Unseen braces and brackets
lift life level to level,
way up high where praise is born.

Rise to Comfort

Full moon soon completes a cycle.
Springtime waltzes its joyful
troubles-be-damned tradition
until time to jitterbug on to June.

I wish I knew what fortune lies ahead.
I'd rock and roll, smile and laugh,
beauty the trails of life, let dreams
fulfill what life leaves undone.

Warm voices call to calm when evening
comes, soothe a body after this long day
takes toll and tide. Welcome this time,
this bide until the great empty cries again.

Where is the voice to soothe the night?
Hear those oak trees speak from trunks of time.
Expectations intertwine with scattered bluets,
wild among tea herbs and iris, rise up to comfort.

My Handmade House

Well laid in décor, this house is a mess.
Most of the time life happens in scraps
and notes. Memorabilia weaves
with fine threads far into future,
potpourri of plan and improvisation.

A long maple table tells stories,
the life of trees, their uses and their beauty.
Budgets, letters, homework, quick bites
of soup and sandwich or bright elegant
feasts of joy breathe the heart wood grain.

Six chairs hold cushions of comfort,
vibrant highs of indigo and burgundy
or fitful spells of hope and despair,
depths gone purple and blue.
Triple candelabra lights a centerpiece

of berries, pinecones, and fiddle-fern,
directs a breath out the doors and windows,
where nature sets sun on tree limbs
fresh or broken, and fields of disordered grass
grow crazy wild, edible or untouchable.

Squirrels and wood thrush share birdfeed.
Earthworms crawl deep dirt, uninhibited.
Final drops of rain fall soft, glisten off
the daily fear. Sunshine finds its way
to the house where scraps and notes
write beauty, and outside finds the way in.

May

When one wild azalea sparks blooms of bright
orange clusters down by the springhead
and bumblebees buzz around white droplets
of blueberry flowers still alive after a late freeze,

the giant pileated woodpecker pounds
a message home. Wipe off the fears
of winter now. Watch yellow butterflies
flit through the breeze, find a smile to follow.

Spy a lucky horseshoe nailed to the mule shed.
Squat down to sit where the dogwood blooms
and sunshine splays warm, and daydreams
come close enough to touch.

Tradition

Molasses works well. Brown the sugar.
Follow an old recipe step by step.
Separate yolks from egg whites,
measure the butter, scald the milk.

Remember stories taught young,
let one part kindle another,
smile big and laugh out loud.

Butterscotch tastes best
when sunshine finds the window
on a clear winter morning.

Stir constant with the old wooden spoon,
don't stray away from the stove.
When it looks done let it chill in the fridge.

Walk the lane while butterscotch sets.
Take comfort from frost-covered blades green
rising from brown dirt older than time.

Return to the voice of a friend,
bowls glazed with memory,
buds of taste untarnished by time.

Together

A communion of friends fans flames,
zest of light and joy near nests of bluebirds
where eggs hatch into new-born feathers,
fly the sky and come back to tell.

Pine trees grow new needles and limbs.
White-green stands of branches-to-be
stand straight up like candlesticks,
kindle life, hope, plans for more.

When the dear ones move cross country,
live closer to home, the world will embrace
the place, carve kindness with strokes of ease,
gather the clan, expected or not.

Sit then on the front porch steps with me
when the sun comes up over the mountain.
Watch the world begin again and again.

Forever

Moon past full, something ended,
something else starts afresh.

Crows call, woodhen cackles back,
a cotton tail runs across your path.
Beardtongue and daisy fleabane,
common below majestic dogwood in bloom,
buttercups and johnny-jump-ups fill
space underfoot.

You follow two black dogs down
to the creek, watch forever fall over rocks,
past familiar, out to an unknown sea.

Strong Bones

Strong bones of life endure storms,
thunder rolls and rumbles, wind with wails
and water rise to pulse, trial after trial.

Listen when the journey finally speaks
slow, late drizzles of rain in early dusk.
Frogs croak loud, crickets strum along.

All the world's away. This pine porch keeps
a steady solitude. Time passes, invites
the dark to sit in a chair next to light.

Memories struggle, blood against bone,
dead set to shirk off fear, walk the unknown
path tomorrow and tomorrow.

Apple Pie and Kindness

Slice these apples, peeled and pared.
Cut careful, for a special kindness done.

Mix sugar, cinnamon, flour. Set aside.
Make a crust from scratch, roll gently,
keep kindness in mind.
Quickly place crust into a pie pan,
not too much touch.

Scoop half the apple slices,
cover the crusted bottom,
sprinkle half the sugar mix,
last half of the apples, end with sugar,
love in each layer.

Top with three tabs of butter,
then crown with crust.
Pinch the edges closed.
Forty minutes in your oven
at four hundred degrees is enough.

Serve with thanks and smiles
for a special kindness done.

II

Early Springtime at Home

Birdsong pleasures this early morning. Cool
soon after dawn, Sally Belle stands far out
in her mule pasture, steady fixture to hold me
in the days of change. Dogwoods still pure white
with flower. Azaleas bright red and soft purple
domesticate the yard. Spring green smiles
the trees, almost naïve, youth of the season.
First wild cherry blooms dangle surprise today.

Alive in Spring

Sun starts soft, then breaks to brilliant, blue sky
boasts big into beams. Little violets volunteer
for beauty anywhere they please, yard and field.
Grass grows greener today than yesterday.

Dogs at play, tree frogs sing, birds fly wherever
they want. Woodpeckers tap tunes in the cedars.

That ancient maple tree wears red tips of spring,
first start of full flora, best shade tree in the field.

Grand displays, blooms of pear, apple, forsythia
pride their peak. Daffodils fade slow, iris soon
to bloom. Mountain mint grows wild in clumps.
Bloodroot blooms white all over the mountain.

Stop and speak to Sally Belle mule, queen of the
meadow. She lives alone now. Honor the grief
for all who no longer walk the springtime path.

Dog Named Magic

Magic, the bright-eye, jumpy foot, little black dog visits
the neighbors, turns them into extended family, naps
on their couch, gets petting from farmer-man hands.

Canine wise, he keeps us together, beyond the passing
wave of a hand along the road we all drive every day.

He runs ahead, not next to me, on my morning walks,
takes charge in these times of change.

Wild touch-me-nots grow tiny orange petals, big
straggles and clumps. Brown-eyed-Susans bright
roadside edges like sunshine itself. Deep in the wood,
chanterelle mushrooms wait for wild forage,
good eating for supper tonight.

Rose Creek begins to clear after weeks of storms
and rain. Rocks keep steady in these moving waters.
Times change and still stay the same.

A red-tailed hawk flies the sky in this cove as always.
Deer still dance the field in starlight, and the little dog
sleeps still by the front door till morning comes again.

After Dogwood Winter

What happens to Solomon Seal and Catesby's Trillium
when their short season ends? Common daisy fleabane,
beard tongue and buttercup last longer, thrive before
clover takes over.

White pines spring up pale tips of new growth.
Even the walnut sports her full-leaf crown
of green. My old black dog rolls into a full backflip
down the field, scratches to satisfy, then runs, perky,
sway of sass in her hips, empress for another season.

What does the earth do when it wants more tender
and more gentle? Do birds sing simply for the fun?
How does anyone ease away from fear? Be like
birds, fly trusted spans between heaven and earth.

New Ways from Old

Grief saturates the land like midnight rain,
soaks what once were worn parched
places, casts a spell of anguish, languish,
loss, argue, and resent, then lays eggs
on the one who rests in peace, to hatch
new ways from old, so love and trust
have space to grow, to live in peace.

Tale of the Pink Lady Slipper

When daisies bloom white petals with God's-eye
centers in the field and under the mule fence, look
down the woodland edge, where wood fairies dance
and sing. Look for pink blooms like moccasins
between folds of wide green leaf.

In the old days, back when bliss blew on every breeze,
this woodland edge, low in the dappled shade, poplar
and pine, pink lady slippers would bloom every year
in the right light, right soil, the right love in the air.

Back then, cheers rose every year at this time, hugs
and smiles, always expected, still always surprise
and wonder, pink puffs of blooms. It was as though
life sustained love and love sustained light and soil.

In time, trees thinned by other forces, light changed,
and love thinned, eroded. No elixir could quench
this thirst for change.

In the year following the change, pink lady slipper
did not appear, never yet to return. Birdsong tradition
says the rare bloom only grows where love grows
full, free, bright as sun and stars.

Wood fairies still dance and sing, call for love to grow
and thrive. The old one believes the signs. When pink
lady slipper flowers again in this woodland edge,
love returns to live.

Beauty by Surprise

Look how this blue-eyed grass comes back
year after year,

wild, unplanted, undisturbed in nature
year after year,

scarce blue star in the ground among the green
startles with simple beauty, same spot
year after year.

Sifting Kindness

Kindness plowed this garden,
harrowed clumps to smooth.

Good rich dirt does the healing
when sorrow suddens into view,
silts the sights, tilts the sky.

Flowers find food in soil,
sprout leaves, burst into bloom
alongside sad and worry.

Kindness and dirt mend most things.
Plant new were old growth failed.
Last night's rain relieves a strain.

Daisies and buttercups thrive
in a field where no one plants.

Drag a hoe through the soil now,
carve garden rows with ease,
then sow seeds, Tenderette beans,
crookneck squash, okra and corn.

Love and luck will grow this garden
where weeds take second place
and kindness sifts dirt to smooth.

Flow in Place

Rain comes along in its own time,
expected or not, sunshine the same.

Try to know how the world works,
ask questions, wait for answers.
Dizzy lets go its hold, muddy water runs
clear at last. Tangled masses and blurs
of confusion un-do, emerge a pattern.

Rose Creek knows to flow south.
Everything else flows in place.

Now this indigo bunting lands on the feeder,
only seen in quick darts of flight for years.
Privileged now, gaze on this pure blue hue
until flight takes its way again.

Spring Rain

When you smell spring rain coming
and a big storm is brewing, creeks hurry
over rocks and logs, and rush their way
to wherever water loves to go.
Birds sing high, shriek mad alerts,
ready for serious change.
An owl calls an eerie *Who-o-o*
right in the middle of day.
Rabbits run and the cow lies down
in the grassy green field.
Farmers head to the house
and the puppies follow right behind.
Still the dogwood stands at half bloom,
full dignity of the season.

The Storm

Save some water in the big blue pitcher. Fill
a few glasses too. This storm's swelling up fast,
wind threatens windows, rafters and me.

Sure enough, the power goes off. Reach for a little
red flashlight. Four messages come in from the county,
tornado warning, then a siren screeches an alarm.

Almost midnight. Grab a pillow, make space, sit under
the kitchen stairway, safe away from windows. Read
with small light beam, pass the hour.

Later, a prayer of thanks. All is well here where I live.
Sleep the dark away until morning sun shines to wake
the world. Walk outside to greet the trees still standing.

Good Year for Little Violets

Purple petals lay low all over this green
field. One pileated hollers his hello, deep
in the trees. Forsythia glows like gold
and maples show off their early red
until majestic green sets the season.

Sally grazes the mule field, no shortage
of early spring grass, no need to eat
the little violets.

Puppy dogs bark between a constant hum
of cicadas. Pairs of birds begin to chirp.
My footsteps are the only human sound.

Wildflowers

Pick flowers for myself before hard beats
of rainfall pound down on purple petals,
then tie the bouquet with a ribbon from my hair.
Field rabbits watch, nod their cotton tails,
and red birds sing me all the way home.
Flower aromas fill my small cabin all day long.

Father's Day

Daddy, I'm into things today that you would do,
hired a handy man for some of it, repairs I don't
know, or lack the strength, now that age adds on
to age.

We could have painted this picnic table together,
instead of me alone. You'd like how it turned out,
simple practical white, solution to weathered
pine boards.

My kitchen faucet has no wiggle now, stays
in place, hot or cold, whatever the use of this sink
of withered time that used to be yours.
The screen door out back has no rips, good as new,
really looks up-town. I think you'd smile.

I see your blue eyes in the afternoon sky, look up
in the direction you might be now.
I hope you're still proud of me, Daddy. Your pat
on the back always made life better, no matter
the rest.

On the Farm

My walk saturates me with a love this mountain
cove always offers.

A neighbor's rooster roams the cove. This game-cock
seeks places away from home, ventures half a mile
away, finds grass, grains and berries not yet ripe.

Clumps of daisies grow together, honeysuckle vines over
and over itself, starts a sweet fragrance. Daylilies smile
big orange blossoms. A mother of ducks walks her chicks,

travels along Rose Creek, waddles in tall weeds where rain
swells the overflow. Hear them jabber their quack-quack,
meander across the road to visit the lonely brown cow.

Weeds want to grow in good dirt, space where asparagus
wants to thrive. Pull up long-root dock, blades of grass,
thin out new stalks of corn so each has room to grow.

Mesmerized with nature's wily subtle way, basked in rain
and sun, fill baskets, wild greens and garden vegetables.
Make best friends with trees, walk beneath a rich canopy.

Late morning mist rises, reveals Flea Mountain in a cloud.
Down on the ground red clover flowers.

Honor

Lavender and petunias are gone,
fall the way of the long shovel.
Worker men come to dig, puzzle,
solve slogs, clogs and breaks into solution.

A third crew comes after my pleas
to please remember I'm a neighbor,
two miles down our country road,
children in school together long ago.
Almost on my knees, I beg
my neighbor to speak up for me,
tell the boss's dad *I'm one of us,
do not ignore my troubles please.*

One portion of the fix and then another
slowly get done between other jobs after work.
Surprises and re-calibrations rule the routes
of effort. Masters of quick thinking and experience
make this world work, no matter the mess.

Meanwhile, hummingbirds sip nectar
from purple bee balm in sunshine.
Stately trees live past their own breaks,
all in harmony with birds and squirrels.

After the fix is finished, sun shines bright,
beams intense rays on clods and crevices,
earth still on the mend where rabbits run the field.

Marvel and Wait

Plant new flowers where old ones failed to do,
push through obstacles, veils of disappointment.
Even nature plays by surprise.

Follow the rush when a sweet smell of honeysuckle
feeds adventure, begs to live wild without bound.
Marvel at garlands of blackberry flowers soon to fruit.

Watch while the farmer cuts his first hay.
See two mourning doves fly, spread secrets
for those who understand.

Search mines of memory, follow underground paths
like earthworms and hidden vein of precious stone.
Be the hound who trusts trail, ground, and scent.

When blurs of pain prevail, walk the piney woods,
stand still where the ancient Merlin tree stands tall.
Wait for magic to enter the door of a hollow chamber.

III

Slow

Wake up zombie-tired,
wait to be moved.

Soft bird songs slip
long silence between notes,

procession this daily walk
to Rose Creek Falls.

White clover fades fast,
young-springtime goes down.

Queen Anne's lace blooms now,
starts up hot days of summer.

Slow strawberry moon grows
towards full.

Morning Prayer

Past the heat wave, cool summer mornings,
grab a jacket. Walk up the mountain path,
only a symphony of birds for companions.

And when the morning sun shines golden
through the beech tree branches, stop a moment
in the glimmer before you walk on.

Praise the daisies. Give medicine to the hemlock
out back, try to keep life alive.
Wait for berries to blue, ripe and ready,
hope the mummy berry fungus sleeps all summer.

Beautiful Wild

Foam flowers rise white between clumps
of faded purple phlox. Birds chirp high
in the hardwood canopy. Big sunshine
tops the east mountain, filters this rugged
landscape near the mule barn. Nearby
a hayfield stretches wide, not ready to grow.

Rose Creek glistens, gurgles, rushes clean
and clear, changes from little waterfalls
to long smooth flow, on down to forever
out of sight.

Venus looking glass and some invasive
iris perk up purple among roadside
weeds. Even half-dead walnuts green up
in new leaf clusters. Wild blackberries
begin the bloom hither and yon. Spots
of orange show up among the brush, native
flame azalea.

Branches of a giant beech tree sprout full
dress of spring green, rugged royalty
in the front yard of a long empty house.

Summer

Get in the flow. Wear purple. Waste a little time.
Watch hummingbirds and buntings
land on the feeder. Get a close look.

Giggle when water flow and mechanicals
work in a good wave.
Wrestle with technology when it's unfit for life.

See the sun rise right there where the moon
comes up at night. Marvel and wonder about nature,
expected precision between surprises.

Laugh into sudden drops falling off trees in a breeze,
not really rain.
See two dogs spring ahead, delight in the life of it all.

Eat sugar snap peas for breakfast, straight from vines.
Plant flowers after supper, when the moon is new
and all time begins its flow again.

Before Breakfast

Mulch new flowers early, before sun
gets hot enough for trouble and thirst.

Walk garden rows, check on potatoes, beans,
greens and tomatoes. Praise the good stand
of peaches-and-cream corn.

Berries almost blue, calculate the time till ripe,
cut a hand full of red roses and white daisies.

Love the sunshine after a week of storms,
then pray for rain again when sun blast bakes
the soil and every creature begs for breeze.

Decide

Fresh out of courage, tired to the bone,
looking for the way, one toe at a time:

Make myself useful, dead-head
these petunias, then the roses.
Help little living things
that can't help themselves,

bring flowers to the graveyard
because memories live forever.
Pet the dogs, keep a tender touch.
Give the mule an apple core.

Say "I love you," often if it's true.
Phone an old friend. It feels good,
grows the more you give.
Be the person I'd like to know.

Work when it's dry and rest when rain
pounds hard. Walk where a canopy
of maple trees takes my breath away
every time I pass.

Rest

The call to rest comes on a red bird wing,
drifts deep down into bones and blood,
past mind, past words, past sensibility,
where rhythm and dance reside
but no music plays, not a step to move.
Fear crawls in like secrets, remains a moment,
then retreats.

Put aside everything. Find the vacant space.
Count on the wings of common crows
and the regal red-tailed hawk.
Clear the body, succumb to rest.

Subtle, become like white fairy wands
blooming on the shallow edge
of an untouched forest where deer step careful,
hardly seen or heard.

Listen to the signal for rest, find a space to nestle.
Give in to rhythms natural as a breeze unexpected.

Luck

A young doe stands by the edge of the oak woods,
steps toward me instead of away,
then leaps down the field, leads me home.

Mystic, my deaf dog, turns around time to time,
keeps close watch when we walk,
stays with me when I turn, find a different path.

Big ripe blueberries speak their struggle
with mummy berry fungus, human help to overcome.
All things want what they were born to be.

Mysteries, modern communication complicate the mind,
how plants grow, what gets fixed and what goes fallow.
Non-growers always ask why my berries fail or succeed.

Berries respond when a mummy spore invasion stops
before tiny specks can reach the flowers in spring,
no formula perfects the process to precision.

It is more like falling in love. Be your best.
Get a rhythm, tend with consistency, open to surprise
when fruits appear, never know what will happen.

Instinct

When warblers sing morning songs
and redbirds call to one another,

be the daisy, simple God's eye, bloom wild
along roadsides and masses of clover.

Be a sunflower seed fallen out of the feeder,
flower in surprising places.

Move into the Merlin tree, claim privilege
to home where no one else can live.

Plant yourself like mint. Place with purpose,
spread roots everywhere, wilder the better.

Tending

Onions and carrots in the old soup pot
simmer until time for pieces of herb,
chicken and broth. Health grows
with hugs for a sick friend today.

Garden overwhelms this time of year.
June gnats are bad. Swat and swish,
my hand is a fan in front of my face.

Weeds compete with corn and beans
and drag tomato vines down from stakes.
Half a day's love with hand and hoe,
before rain starts, makes all the difference.

Queen Anne's lace grows in bouquets
along the locust fence. Tiny golden birds burst
into flight, up from a fallow cornfield,
no one alive left to plant.

Blest by fireflies at dusky dark,
later the full moon rises its super-self
over the mountain.

One firefly got in my bedroom, darted
corner to corner in the dark.
When flight stopped its light went out,
moonlight was still there, left as a gift.

Someone's Home

Two gladiolus stalks grow red and gold
in front of this old abandoned house,
near a porch swing, quiet and clean.

Residents long gone, a walnut sapling
sprouts mid-porch, floor to roof.
One naked light bulb hangs from a wire,
waits for electric fire to light up the entry.

Rusted clothesline poles still stand
by the corn patch now crammed with weeds.
An old TV antenna stands unwired, replaced
by a satellite dish facing east.

Roof shingles still perfect, siding only faded,
and an enormous homemade daisy decoration
above the doorway, say massive love lived here.

Deep in Summer

I

Birds chirrup cheerful early this cool mountain morning,
before cars and tractors make a sound, before full sun
cracks open that layer of cloud. Sourwoods bloom high.
A lazy creek flows low under the county bridge.

Stop walking now. See that mass of brown-eyed-Susans
up the hill, simple beauties to start the day with love.

II
Smells of fresh mowed field grass
fill the ground, lift me high.
Leftover rain waits for more.
Crows fill the early morning air.
Brush fires flame late, magic
laces dusky dark before the stars
come out to spend the night.

III

Yellow flowers will grant garden squash,
crookneck, eat raw or cooked quick.
Wait for ripe, wait for the time.

Bluebirds lay their eggs in a wooden house
on a pole in the field. Wait the time, tiny
birds, if no danger lurks and takes.

Wait for water, come to boil. Wait for a baby
to be born. Wait for time that minds itself.
Clouds swell, wait for rain or storms.

Wait for what stirs inside, soul to rise,
ideas to voice, words to speak, songs to swell
over and over and over again.

My Son Says I'm a Plant Maniac

I call the names of common plants I know,
wonder about others in mudflats,
wetlands, dunes, playgrounds, yards.

Curious about variations of sage and daisy,
I find genus and species, local names
and descriptions, while my son ignores,
mind on math problems and rock climbing.

Once a plant maniac, always a plant maniac
he says, a smile to exaggerate
the difference between mother and son.
One look, and that smile, we both time travel back
to wildflower walks in pristine forests
paired with games of catch, trail start to finish.

Today we feast where we both love the food,
walk through neighborhoods new to us,
raise a glass to life that develops unexpected,
and even maniacs never
find names for the treasures.

Hope

Move these rocks and bricks, stack well,
sturdy hold for future need.
Catch up on chores, mow grass, trim bushes.
Straighten papers, clear space for pride
and comfort next to places at the table.

Gather friends and food. Clean from rain,
the whole world looks better now.
Sourwoods bloom, nectar for the queen
of mountain honey, Appalachian grown.
Orange butterfly weed pops up wild in green grass,
says deep summer is here. Hot days direct
short rests in the shade,
and cool down comes late in the night.

Keep life with tradition, fresh flowers, garden greens.
Mix music old and new.
Soon the young will return.

Wonder

Rabbit sits still as an oak on a slope of green grass still
wet with dew, won't move till I walk by, gone from sight.
I wish to stay, stare, side view of one black eye, ears
straight up, brown fur of nature's best.

I wish to be so steady, to keep tradition, protect myself
from daily danger, follow imprint, trusted inner route
to feed, nourish, sustain, a sixth sense along the path.

Meanwhile, the world of wonder lays its spread.
Queen Anne's lace blooms steady, delicate wild
clusters of impulse and joy.

Tomato

Slice the best reddest tomato from the summer garden,
use the sharpest knife in the kitchen, make even rounds
admire color, texture, just juicy enough, get excited,
almost ready to eat.
Slap mayonnaise on two slices of good bread, tomato
slices on top, put it together, bite into the sandwich
you've been waiting for all winter and spring.
Savor in the sunshine, or screened from rain.
Anywhere you call home is where a tomato sandwich
tastes best.

Seeking Chanterelle

Golden chanterelles pop up wild on the forest floor
here in rich dirt, in steamy heat after a soaking rain.

Look for wavy funnels with false gills. Walk slow, find
folds of yellow-orange where sunlight filters in well.

This local wild mushroom grows near hardwood trees
like maple, poplar, and oak, maybe by a white pine.

Take these treasures home, cook in butter with onions,
feast on fine taste, surprise gift of the forest.

IV

Looking for Carolina Asters

This low fog in the cove hides human fault,
highlights nature's wiles and wonders.

Fallen locust fence posts and barbed wire
strung in straight lines be-damned,

goldenrod rises regal this year,
bigger and brighter than always.

Queen Anne's lace nears its end.
Mystery and magic still draw me to this land.

Life falls in and out of place. Here, people
live on farms, as in olden times, no other way

to feed and shelter except by do-it-yourself
brute strength and skill learned father to son.

Every autumn, the purple Carolina asters bloom
wild violet star-bouquets on tangles of stems

in un-mowed places all over this wide cove
until today, in these odd changes of our time.

Bold and Determined

Jewelweed holds its orange petals until bites of frost
claim all parts, back to source.
Dogwood leaves cycle slow, color shift toward red.
Earth turns its seasons. Insecure times, cruel marks
of man, bitter taste, do not quench the season, not yet.

Shame and ridicule mark my story, alter dreams
and visions, never kill the source, never dry
the springhead. Visions always flow with water.
Stronger dreams emerge from struggle. Passion
for purpose defies ties and bounds of reason.

Scorn and torment pop up seldom now, older
in these fermented times. Less afraid, still
marked by shame, miracles grow like flowers
in the wild. Pick a bouquet every day,
celebrate the turn away from binds that cut.

Watch the young deer, tawny one-point buck.
Bold, he stands close, dares to stare, invites you
to admire, waits long, so you will know him.
See, he runs his sister to the wood for protection,
then returns, determined to watch you again.

Foggy Mountain Morning

Ironweed stands tall, pristine purple flowers
tower strong above orange dots of jewelweed
sparkles on tangled vines, wild and delicate.

Cicadas call all morning, drone on without start
or stop. Flocks of goldfinch glow the grey day,
fly the trees, then land on a wire, rule the field.

Sudden rustle in the woods says a deer hides near
in the trees and brush. He scampers deeper behind
bark and leaf, away from my footsteps.

Last stalks of lavender lobelia color clumps
of faded field grass. Rose of Sharon's pink petals
share space with Queen Anne's lace, star of the field.

Tiny white morning glories vine-wrap tall stalks
of ragweed. Summer clings to signs of fall.

Sally the mule stands near her barn. Flea Mountain
peaks above one wide swath of fog.

Moon

I'm outside to see the waning moon.
Below, Orion's belt shines bright
among sparkles of stars I know well
but never met by name.

Coyotes call from the mountain ridge.
Night crickets hum soft repeats,
click-a-clack, click-a-clack. Magic
sleeps on his cushion, deep in canine
comfort as if morning will never arrive.

Peaceful is the way on this porch step
where the southern sky opens wide,
reveals moon and stars. Turn by turn,
they offer me a place down in this world.

Death

Grief comes in low whisper or loud holler, echoes
sounds, repeats in the lonely place where breaks
and chasms come out from hiding, claim tears
and attention, write 'helpless' across the days,
take the peace away from night.
Hearts-a-bustin' bloom for times like this.
Autumn leaves sparkle color as they go down.

Summer's Gone

Go straight outside to trees, weeds,
birds and wind. Learn ways unspoken,
be human to the best.

One blue jay lands on a walnut
branch, gets a beak-full of beetle,
flits down to ground, deep in brush,
near a wetland dammed up by beaver
last spring.

Some of my friends don't speak
to each other anymore. Others make
way, forget hard hearts and unfair times.
Autumn leaves wander as they fall.

Down on the hearts-a-bustin' trail,
red pods pop open, boast of beauty.
One honeysuckle still flowers
in a patch of weeds. Carolina asters
come late, full purple bloom today.

Fall in love with a big beech tree,
still full green leaf, immense.
He can hold us all in his arms.

Choose the love of trees, no matter
the stress. Consider squabbles
and spats as misunderstandings.

Butterflies still fly the breeze,
orange and yellow leaves dance
below the bluest sky ever seen.

Thistle stalks already turn black.
Death dares to take someone
you hope not to lose, not yet.

An owl came this morning,
Crows call all day. Chimney
smoke and wildflowers
held in hand will ease the way.

Daybreak

Cold and still, not a breeze to rustle red
and gold leaves high on maple and oak limbs.
A rooster crows far off in the cove.

Mounds and rounds of change mark
this world, still only one me to be,
and I am not done.

Two yellow blossoms still thrive on tomato
plants, survive a dip to thirty degrees
three times. Purple flowers still look fresh
on eggplant stems. These petals will not
have enough warm hours to complete a cycle
to fruit, but I won't pull them up till they turn
black, prove they are done.

Like me, they defy expectations, never live
within the lines and bounds prescribed.
Now I gather split dry oak from the shed,
stack near my cast iron wood stove, lay
paper and kindling, ready to light tonight,
warm flames for the coldest night of fall.

Go Back Outside

Cleaning up the mess, one corner at a time,
one room worse than another, time casts a shadow.
So much to do, never stay on task 'til finish.

How does nature keep house among roots, trunks,
branches, space for sun, shade, always surprise?
A kingfisher darts the air, calls the world to attention.
One purple aster stands still warm down the creek bank.

Cleaning out the bad, used up, gaudy, in-the-way precious
used-to-be's, past boredom, down to raw nerves and bone,
it's time something's got to change in here.

Take a break. Go outside. Watch a family of deer run
through the clean clear frost-covered field, never a noise.
See crystal sparkles on icy flakes where sun streaks glow.

Back inside, clean conscious and steady. Sort stuff
into piles of keep, toss, give. Cut through clutter.
Wash, wipe, rearrange.

Outside again, a stately tree of ragged brown tells me,
Stand back, stare till every crevice of my beauty
magnifies in your eyes. Memorize my bark, my branches,
season by season. Stroll west to the creek where water
runs with rock and wisdom. Then stop in every light
to visit me. Humans need houses for shelter,
but I love you more.

Winter Sun

Stretch out in the strong sun rays
while warm still fills the yard.
Soon, autumn turns our world to winter.
Claim some outside rest while you can.

The neighbor's pasture still shows green
blades of summer. Signs say winter
already begins to step in. A night of killing
frost turned field and bushes white as snow.

Chickadees chirp loud, cardinals keep silent.
Late asters hold tall, still purple. Thistle,
once lavender, turns to floss, then faded scrap.
Queen Anne's lace finally falls to dust,
goldenrod still bright, even if half gone.

Magic, my little dog, speeds along the lane,
scurries around a hollowed-out tree trunk.
Fairies live there, if you pretend to believe.
Rose Creek flows through time, current
stretches out far, glistens in the sun.

Sprout a Plan

For my son

Taste water from a spring deep in the ground,
life with more trees than houses, more animals
than people, space enough to wander provides a certain
peace of mind. Be still until ingenuity sprouts a plan.

Eat from the garden, cultivate soil with hand tools,
plows and tillers. Pull weeds whenever you walk by.
Let dirt, rain, sun, and changing climate guide
decisions for how to live and work today.

Tomorrow, when you travel far away, adventures,
jobs and time will guide your steps, pace your plans,
shout new definitions of home and comfort. Always
the taste of good water will tap your roots, define
each step, sprout a plan when you are far away.

Green sprouts of spring and colored leaves of fall
walk the way, sunbeams bright the sky, part the fog.
Again today in your own home, fresh water tastes good.

Thankful

White tails prance across the field.
Sally the mule stands at my fence,
and birds call for a new day to begin.

Spots of red, gold, and yellow still show
against a world of grey bare tree trunks
with almost empty branches.

Golden beech leaves still cling
long and fast to great outstretched arms
strong enough to hold this world.

Leaves of one white-oak dry brown on the tree,
reddish blends of sourwood fade slow.
Pines, cedar, and holly hold green forever.

Wild turkeys roam the open place,
trot into the woods for cover
as I walk by this corner of winter normal.

The white tail deer dance the field.
I tromp through layers of fallen
leaves, walk the land that holds me dear.

I promise to be good, pet the dog, speak
to neighbors, sign my name on this day,
and allow this land to reveal its secrets.

Walk with Magic the Dog

Magic dog jump-dances his short silly legs,
climbs air-tunnels up by my knees. We start
the morning walk, a natural laugh, adventure

every step of mud puddle gravel under the fog
drenched sky before the next rain, past Sally
the mule who lives outside no matter what

weather may come, past houses where chimney
smoke floats slow, channels up the heavens,
signals all's well and warm in the world we walk.

V

Early Fall Walk

Purple ironweed sparks a majestic mass
of blooms in the weeds. Virgin's Bower
clings, covers, cascades atop weeds high
and low, graceful as a bridal veil.

Tiny orange jewelweed flowers show
their glow between every growing green.
Lavender thistles rise on tall stalks,
turn bristles into beauty.

My little black dog trots his short legs,
pads the familiar path home. One spider
web claims half the porch view. Blue sky
smiles a change of hue, air feels like fall.

Getting Warm

Thinking about firewood, stacks of oak and maple,
floor to roof in the shed, split, dry and ready.
Thinking of how cold it's going to be.

Carry armloads to the front porch rack, some inside
for convenience. Bring a bucket of kindling too.
Cold enough, first fire in the old wood stove tonight.

Bright sun warms the afternoon, easy heat inside
from the great south window. But tonight, stoke
the wood stove, ready to light with a kitchen match.

Warm the apple cider. Bring on the pie and popcorn.
That north breeze is gonna whistle up, grab the dark,
dance with the wind, and freeze the world tonight.

Autumn

Distance gathers. Garden grows sparse,
bend to pick the final few green beans.
Hope for more tomatoes to ripe. Pull
weeds and dead flowers. Clear creeks
of fallen sticks and branches.

Honor spaces of empty, even sunbeams
seem farther apart. The walking path
looks wider, where neighbors cut down
the dying tree. Sally Belle mule lets me
pat her head, closer now, change in the air.

Mule in the Field

Cold morning, Sally Belle stands tall
in the field, a beauty in her sleek brown
coat. Watch her bend easy, nibble green
grass and good wild greens.

Carolina aster still thrive the edges
here under the deep blue autumn sky.

Frost will visit late this year. One
Queen Anne's Lace still stands perfect
on the roadside slope.

Teachers

This earth keeps me, tends
me morning and night.

This walnut tree leads my way,
wild asters teach me beauty
unexpected.

Sally Belle mule nibbles fresh
October greens natural in the field,
endures weather and seasons
with ease.

Beautiful Brown Pair

Sunny the new brown mule joins Sally Belle
today. Neighbor farmers brought her an hour
ago, see if she works out well here. Both
in the old oak barn, Sally Belle lets me pat
her head because we know each other well
by now. Sunny's already eager for my hand,
pokes her head out far as she can, then asks
for more. I hope she stays, runs the field
with Sally Belle.

Companions

I

Love the morning light when dark starts night
so early. Sally Belle and Sunny Girl don't care.
Their field is green, slotted oak stall dry and warm,
feed bins full of fresh hay, good care from farmers.

Two healthy work mules live here, get things done,
pull the wagon when time for fun. Neighbors gather
round, celebrate. Sally Belle has a companion.

Roosters cockle, sun comes out to shine hours past
yesterday's rain. Rose Creek gurgles on.
We all make friends with change.

II

Sally Belle and Sunny Girl munch
hay. Fresh air feeds my feet, mind,
spirit. Every move adventures the day,
spells ways of joy.

Walk past frost-bit goldenrod, then the fresh
cut field. Step on down to Rose Creek.
Watch eddies and ripples of clear water glisten,
rush on to somewhere. Make a wish.

Shaking the Blues

Carry on, as if acquainted with the night to come.

Live and carry on, become the wide river. Flow
on and on, over rocks, under boulders. Determine
to go. Gurgle with pride, glisten in joy.

Learn from regal Sally Belle mule who walks alone
again, head held high, until she bends low to nibble
clumps, best fescue in the field.

Somber on util smiles and grins return. Plant seeds
of joy in rows. Water often, praise every new sprout.
Dance the season with sunshine and raindrops.

Bless the last blushing red rose on the bush before
the hard winter freeze.

Walking

Two deer stand in the field out my front door, stare,
assess for danger, like they might stay. A moment
passes, then they leap, sudden-gorgeous, graceful
leap back into the dark woods.

Along my path, Sally Belle munches hay, stands
in her worn wooden mule stall, lets me pat her head,
seems lonely. But I don't know, we all live the best
lives we can.

Watch the water flow down Rose Creek. Ripples
and gurgles mesmerize, inspire under cold clouds.
I walk back home past final sparkles of morning dew.
Sun shines a bright promise then leaps back into dark.

When Opportunity Calls

Try hard, jump up, dive down into deep water again.
Squeeze both eyes shut. Hold nose tight. Scared
to go, scared not to go. Go anyway.

Unexpected, sun breaks through morning clouds,
shines the way after a perilous dark unknown.

Grass grows. Early flowers bloom wild in fields
and woods. Mules munch dry hay until fescue thrives
in the pasture. Always find a way.

Birds speak unknown tongues, still I treasure the sound.
This farm holds me steady, even after I swim deep or fly
the sky all day with birds, still never know how.

Light

This evening light, after days of rainfall,
and before dark comes on full, shines
its streaks straight down to yellow
daffodils. For a moment, petals turn golden.

Soon the clouds part, turn pale pink.
Deep blue sky appears in patches. Night
glows util too dark to see the last tree
branch shining. Dark finally settles
the world into sleep. The moon comes
over the mountain late, brilliant light
touches down on garden, grass, and rocks.

After night hours finish, morning rises.
A rooster crows. Sally Belle stands tall
in the south pasture. Sun breaks up
the clouds. Blue skies play all day now,
in this place apart, where light always
shines a way.

Living as Things Are

Behind a barbed wire fence, Sally Belle mule
has the field to herself. She lies in grass
to scratch her back, wiggles and nuzzles
her way around and around, wears the grass
out in a ring, sits in the circle she scraped,
cozy nest of dusty brown dirt.

Red and black pileated woodpecker cackles
a call, flies by in a rush.

Brown feathered chickens trot the yard,
walk the road, lift those skinny legs and those
feet like forks, every step a purpose, cross the road
to get to the other side. One web-footed duck
joins as friends in the sun.

Yellow butterflies travel the air, glide currents
on a wisp and a wing. The old walnut tree
stands straight as always.

VI

Cardinal Flower

Red stalks rise from a shallow stream,
blush the gray morning before rain
sets in to rule. Petals of red paint
the land, distract from gnats
who dark the mood, poke the eye,
blur the way.

Magic the tiny black dog races,
rocks and reels his spurts of happy,
gust of surprise, like red wildflower
blooms in the water.

Now the dogwood starts to red.
Watch the leaf tips turn day by day.
Swamp willow weeps for summer's end.
Goldenrod grows in the dry, shines bright,
lights the way to a time yet to come.

Sally the Arabian mule munches field grass
under the locust post barb wire fence.
Time moves slow, and cardinal change
is not yet seen where red sparkles in the gray.

At Home

Two young deer, one-point bucks, show up two mornings
in my south field, been here before when they were fawns.
Gentle, cherish my good fortune, I keep the news to myself.
Innocents like these grow fresh love and fortune,
lure new adventures even in my mind, here at home.

After they turn back to the woods to hide, do their life,
I do mine, hoe vegetables before rain starts, pull weeds,
cut back overgrown bushes and plants, pick berries,
bake a pie, read a book, then back outside.

Later the sun beats hard. Fresh cut hay dries flat
in the upper field. Beads of sweat pour down
every body part like buckets and buckets.
Sun sets when day's work is done.
Dark seeps in slow, invites cool relief.
Deer return in the magic hours. Perfect peace.

An Old Dog

These days when she rallies, walks
her spirited trot, steps close enough
to keep secure, I think Mystic still
has months to live right here with me
even if she's confused, can't hear at all,
can't see much, even in weight drop,
hair loss, stiff bones and strange moles,
and so much sleep. But today's high pitch
shriek when lost on our familiar lane speaks
pain and confusion, sparks my own fear,
tells me to help her rest now, wait for time.

Numbered Days

Stop the old dog from so long a walk, even in the breeze
when whispers of bird-song call me to the birch tree,
down creek-side to the bridge where water tells secrets.

It's as though this dog has my genes. Push on past all,
push on for want, don't miss a thing that might delight.

Watch her perk up now, after a long rest. Instinct intact,
natural curiosity drives her to the pond to bend and drink
until satisfy becomes relax, content for sunrays on her back.

Next burst of joy, explore favorite haunts around the farm,
nose around for bones and bugs to claim. Notice the pride
of her careful scavenge and discovery.

Remember the smelly roadkill pelts she used to carry home
like Christmas gifts, and wildlife bones she dragged down
for all day chews in the grass by rows of blueberry bushes.

Cherish the times when she held silent hope, faithful sitter
through every hardship of the years.

Mystic of the Farm

Cardinal flower blooms crimson on the creek,
rose pink beautifies our ragged roadside.
Crows eat berries too high to reach,
blue skinks dash from porch to post,
gold finches delight the air, fly close
to nibble sunflower seed at the feeder.

Keep watch on every living thing,
pull weeds, pick beans, watch grass grow.
The end is near, Mystic the black lab mix
is old, bad off, getting worse. Plan the way,
help her move, manage her pain, let her go
down easy, whatever turns the curve.

Losing Mystic

Seems like losing another husband.
I fix meals, serve drinks, albeit water
in a bowl on the tile floor, find ways
to make her comfy. She sits near,
knows my moves, my laugh, my tears.
She walks all my walks.

Younger, she kept watch when pneumonia
kept me down, until finally we walked again.
Now older than old, she hears nothing,
sees little, lost to confusion. Leaving me now,
kind needle in her vein, she does not flinch,
only surrenders to comfort, final breath,
on her way to wherever good dogs go.

After Rest in Peace

Sally snorts loud, starts up morning like a motor. Sally
the mule lost her mate, looked lonely at first, now shoots
out the doorway of the old battened barn to graze all day
on summer's green grass.

Now Magic the tiny dog and I walk by ourselves, take
the long way down to the cow pasture, walk quiet paths
early while storm clouds linger past their time. Shade
still claims its privilege. Later the sun comes on strong,
stretches long arms of rays, hot hold on every living thing.

Have you ever had something grab hold, not let go, drive
you on? That strong call, need to go, get on with life, long
ago and still today, the kind that picks you up, turns
you dizzy, plops you down wild in some idea, won't let go
until you do something, even if crazy.

Sally snorts again, re-starts her motor. Life falters,
starts up again, calls and keeps calling one step and then
the next, after the dead have found their peace. Life links
breath with some new notion, gives life to a bold new
inspiration. Call of the muse won't let go.

Lessons from Mystic

Haul off on great adventures
even close to home every day.

Rest on the porch in summer,
by the fire in winter.

Eat what is served. Eat with gusto.
Never be afraid to ask for more.

Bark at bad people.
Apologize if you get it wrong.

Greet friends with a smile.
Expect a scratch behind the ear,
kind words in human terms.

Be happy all the time.
Sleep more when you are old.

Be faithful to the end.
Leave peaceful when time is up.

Beginning

Magic jumps, dances *joy of living*, excites the world
again, time for our morning walk. Fifteen pounds,
faster than lightning, this feisty pooch runs ahead
then doubles back, keeps to my heel except to claim
a locust fence post, as boy dogs do.

Sally, the girl mule, stands mid-field below an early
layer of fog, big mouthful of long grass to chew.
Green strands hang out both sides of her mouth till
she sucks it all inside. Not a noise or a breeze distracts
Sally. She swishes her tail, bends for more, jerks
her head to get the gnats away.

Moments on the morning walk, time never moves, birds
sing on forever, no one speaks a word. The world steps
back, then steps ahead again, reaches out a hand of breeze
as if to dance. Next step means *I accept,* and now
this day begins.

Long Summer

Mid-August heat wave breaks.
Lawn mower sputters.
Wait for another day, hope
rest does a motor some good,
same rest that helps a person.

Count cardinal flowers. Tall stalks
of crimson petals dart up sudden
from the skinny creek, stark
majestic rise above fields of fescue.
One shy deer shows in the distance.

Sally nibbles her breakfast greens.
Healthy mule with the shiny coat,
she stares at me, still uncertain.
What bond is worth the chance,
for a mule who lost her best friend?

Rose-pink, black-eyed Susan, and white
Queen Anne's lace balance colors
with green field grass and forest trees.
Tall goldenrod, Joe Pye weed and Virgin's
Bower bloom near a lonely brown cow.

Quartz crystals glow amid gravel stones,
dirt and pebbles, form the rutted road to home.
Two neighbor dogs trot down to visit mine.
One purple bloom of ironweed foretells
the season: fall gold and orange soon to come.

Changes

Quiet in this mist, Sally Belle looks pretty in a southern
lady kind of way, shiny coat, ears perked, tail swish
like all is well with every breeze. She turns, tunes to me,
catches my eye as I walk., stays me with her stare, then turns
her head again quick, bends to munch the big leaf green,
engaged in a world of her own.

She does not know the farmer found the friend she waits
for, another Arabian mule. He's worked out a price, wants
to know now, *Is he able to work?*

Sally waits for her daily hay. Goldenrod and Joe Pye
Weed stand tall in the sun. Days already get shorter,
and the heat wave is over. Rose mallow blooms
in the shallow creek. A hawk flies from my maple tree
across the open air, deep into a poplar grove. I'm waiting
for ironweed to spark majestic blooms of deep purple
when August turns to September.

Fog Lifts

Sun shines now, clears the day.
Say hi to Sally. She stands stately
at the door of her mule stall.

Magic dog acts like himself again,
jumps, bounces, dances his front paws,
excited simply to see me.

No explaining, Rose Creek keeps
steady on with its flow. Brown cow
still grazes the green field.

A neighbor rooster crows the day awake.
One Carolina aster shows its face, perfect
purple, steps me right into fall.

VII

Neighbors

Just a light chill, now morning breaks,
and I walk the lane in early light.
Sally Belle comes to greet
me at her mule fence. I bring

empty egg cartons to the neighbor
with two dogs in the window,
pick up a fresh dozen going home.

Magic, short leg little mutt, scurries
more than runs, visits both houses
nearby, smells bacon on their stoves.

Another day of wonder in the cove, new
ideas meet ancient locust fence posts,
a giant vine grows up a yellow pine,
black crows call claim to the sky,
and the neighbor builds a log bridge
across the creek.

Cranberry Bread

For Mandy

Get the big red bowl, right size for a double batch.
Measure flour, sugar and more, cut butter into the mix.

Rain on the roof makes music. Sing in time with pitter
patter, glance out the window at puddles on the ground.

Chop cranberries and pecans. Crack two eggs, stir
with orange juice and joy. Use the long wooden spoon

to beat the batter till it looks just right. Pour with love
into loaf pans greased and floured, place in hot oven.

Wait for familiar smell to tell you it's almost done.
Smile for Mandy who made this bread a tradition.

Set aside loaves for neighbors and friends. Admire
winter birds as you deliver.

Give a nod to heaven, for rain and all good souls
who still rhythm ways of kitchen breads and kindness.

Thanking Trees

Shade trees and Christmas trees, firewood, lumber,
allure and splendor, the language of trees speaks
beyond purpose, beyond billions of eons and time.

Wild cherry, native Appalachian, calls beauty
every season: long white flowers, full leaf
summer, or bare bone branches against a winter sky.

Choose one great tree, harvest for fine furniture,
turned bowls, or careful carvings of squirrels, owls,
bears and deer. Watch the wood grain reveal and shine
every stroke, shave, and polish. Display with pride,
every perfect piece.

Rally round redbuds and maples where white pines
used to grow. Remember American chestnuts of old.
Rest under a neighbor's beech tree, branches like arms
spread wide to hold us all. Talk to dogwoods
when they flower, berry, and turn red.

Admire a ninety-foot white oak growing in grace year
after year. Look for wildflowers under towers of tulip
poplars close to locust, hornbeam, and hickory. Count
on conifers when others drop leaves in winter. Cut holly
branches, pretty on Christmas when berries turn crimson.

Speak to the eastern hemlock by the lane, the one who
escaped aphids that killed nearly all. Ask advice
for long life. Talk to your ancient walnut now done
and dying. Ask how to manage the years of your life.

***On The Anniversary of My Short Marriage
to a Man who Only Loved My Land***

Today's rain wants to wash away
dark dents, broken limbs,
and night echoes, eerie with truth,
embossed with imagination, secret hopes
stitched together with threads
that never held.

Today's rain rinses dust from leaves
who hold fast. Memories rise,
a tear on one side, fear on the other.

Bark of the maple tree swells, bursts
layers of knife lines, worn out images,
initials carved by marriage now dead.

Today's rain tries too hard, floods the field,
erodes the road. Ditches deepen, expose
errors and blemishes, years of best intent,
love alone honed and polished along the way.

Soon, as season comes to autumn,
a flower called Hearts-a-Bustin'
will bloom bright red in the unkempt sod
in the edge of the road.

Winter

Trees stand stoic. Moss speaks soft
and fragile, even as roots grab strong
fingers underground,
keep a strong hold on the bank.

Walk slow outside this cold winter morning.
The forest talks to those who listen. Learn
the language of woods and trails. Be inspired
by the sky. Quiet winter reveals its truth.

Sweet smell of wood smoke rises from a chimney,
maple logs cured two years warm the house well.

Still Sunshine and Moonshine

In the land where morning sunlight gives gold
to tree leaves of summer, red clover and berries
fill the field where corn used to tower tall,

this old moonshiner's shack, tar paper black, still
stands, never caves in, never fall to ruins of rodents,
mold, or floods from years of leaky pipes.

Many a bottle of liquid gold left Harley's hand, many
a story told on the porch, secrets kept in those times
long remembered and changed.

New owners sweep the yard clean today, replace floors
and posts, cover old tar paper with brand new sheet metal
sides as they unravel history, stories, and smiles.

Now a cock-a-doodle-do still calls the morning, and one
pesky fly still bothers the brown mule. An apple tree still
grows out back, golden delicious.

At dusk, magic fireflies still sparkle low, two whitetail
deer graze the pasture until dark in the moonshiner's cove,
and honeysuckle and hollyhock flower smiles old and new.

December Sun

Go outside. Sunshine swells behind those gray clouds,
faint light seeps through. Now a bit of blue peeks out.

Walk south, past patches of apple green moss in wet
brown leaves down on winter ground. Native hollies
and pines grant color next to barren oak and maple.

Worn out rocks bank the one lane road. Locust posts
of old still hold fence lines for reasons long past.

Now, after weeks of rain, ray after ray of sun reaches
and stretches long bright arms around me,
replaces clouds, smiles a day born to light and joy.

A Natural Glow

Sunshine peeks through the pines,
chimney smoke falls way down
to the ground. It's going to warm
up and rain. Been bleak, icicles
still freeze on the creek bank,
fishpond thins its layer of ice.
Waiting for rain, feeling the warm,
rhododendron leaves finally rise
to an easy angle. Days on end
they pointed straight to the dirt,
nature's way when it's mighty cold.
Green moss clings to soil and rocks.
This great earth keeps wild and crazy,
changes quickly, holds me all the time.

Gone

Lonely cow I've loved
will not walk this field
again, nor graze green
grass, or meet me
by the fence.

Companion in isolation
years, pandemic disbelief,
I'd smile, holler hello, tease
her brown hide close to me,
never matter the fence.
No word, no doubt, she'd
return the feeling her way.

I think I know the cow's fate,
so I don't ask.

Mass of purple periwinkle smile
the ground. Tall maples dress
in early season red. Pairs of birds
sing with the sun. Horses fill
pastures near, but the cow's field
by me is empty.

To Sew the World Into the Life You Own

Take a tiny bite of your own life.
Delve in at one spot. Chew well.

Be like a soft morning mist.
Linger long, leave slow.

Stitch a piece of life to this mountain.
Make it yours.

When trouble comes, hold on
to the mountainside.

Dig your feet and fingers between rocks.
Get a grip. Make your own trail.

Learn every weed, flower, and tree.
Make friends with birds, dogs, and deer.

Sit at night with a friend. Watch two grey fox
slow-walk under giant oak and walnut trees.

Morning brings a flock of turkeys. See
them whoosh, jet by, eye level in flight.

Eat berries and drink from a stream.
Dream under stars. Sunrise starts anew.

Peace

Misty morning near winter solstice, wet
leaf litter lines the path, puddles fill
the middle parts.

Put your feet down careful, walk light
on this good ground. Watch little brown
birds flit the way of early morning routine.

Flirt with trees who wear winter well, keep
close to strong bare limbs or green fir-filled.
Learn to live like these trees.

Speak to Sally Belle mule.
Stand strong like her. Find your place
of peace on this great earth.

Out in the Country

Early, walk the lane at first light, still
cold after a frigid night, mix of late
winter and early spring.

Step this path where life began forty
years ago, when purple phlox fell me
into love with this land, on to build
a house from scratch, reclaim bottom
land from ticks and straw, until topsoil
proved its worth.

Birds sing unseen, high where treetops
reach the heavens. Low blue crocus
and clumps of yellow daffodils bloom
where planted. First sprays of wildflowers
wait, will their own way.

Black Magic, the little dog, runs far
out of sight, then back again, into
a dense mess of forsythia spires, dives
down the creek gorge, back up top,
skirts the locust post fence, looking
for two buckskin mules who moved
away yesterday. Sally Belle, Arabian mule,
stands still, noble queen of the north
pasture, reigns in peace where nature
plays both gentle and brutal.

Late, the young neighbors, quarter
mile up the hill, call at bedtime,
We heard a loud sound. Are you OK?
I didn't hear it. I'm Ok. *Must have been
the other side of the hill. Sounded like
gunshot. Glad you are safe.*

Ways of peace play well out here today.
Sleep comes easy.

Held by Nature

Thank you, birds who call the day,
and morning mist that hangs soft,
quiet, gives a hug.

Thank you, little dog who waits
on the porch, ready to walk
with me awhile.

Thank you, wild turkeys who graze
early in the field and walk across
my road, into safety of the woods.

Thank you, sunglow creeping over
the mountain before full bright.

Thank you, trees who keep standing
in their bark that keeps on holding.

Thank you, honeysuckle in the wild,
where you do no harm to crops
of beans or blueberries.

Thank you, cobwebs in the weeds,
and pretty daisies, red clover,

and buttercups, lovelies strong
enough to survive a brush
with the mower.

Thank you, peaceful sky, as pensive
dark turns to wide-open blue.

Thank you for the way you touch
my tender heart before I brace
to face the world.

Acknowledgments

Mountain Lakes Anthology, 2025, *Early Springtime at Home*

Old Tales Anthology, 2021, *Someone's Home*

Fall and Holiday Anthology, 2024, *Early Fall Walk*

Reach of Song, Anthology of Georgia Poetry Society, 2020, *On The Anniversary of My Short Marriage to a Man Who Only Loved My Land*

Gold Medal, Cherokee County NC, Silver Medal state level, North Carolina Senior Games/Silver Arts, 2024, *Gone*

Gold Medal, Cherokee County Senior Games/Silver Arts 2025, *Held by Nature*

About the Author

Mary Ricketson's poems reflect the healing power of nature, a path she follows rooted in Appalachian tradition, with the surrounding mountains serving as the midwife for her words. *Tall Flowers and Living Long* is a collection of poems written day by day, capturing her life closely intertwined with the natural world.

She is a mental health therapist in private practice in Murphy, NC, and enjoys writing groups, hiking mountain trails, and tending to her garden of vegetables, flowers, and blueberries.

Her published poetry books include *I Hear the River Call My Name*, *Hanging Dog Creek*, *Shade and Shelter*, *Mississippi: The Story of Luke and Marian*, *Keeping in Place*, *Lira - Poems of a Woodland Woman*, *Precious the Mule*, and *Stutters: A Book of Hope*. She won first place in the 2011 Joyce Kilmer Memorial Forest 75th Anniversary National Poetry Contest and earned gold and silver medals for poetry in the 2024 and 2025 Literary Arts division of the NC Senior Games.

Engage with Mary at: www.maryricketson.com

www.ingramcontent.com/pod-product-compliance
Lightning Source LLC
Chambersburg PA
CBHW031136090426
42738CB00008B/1114